ISBN 0-932529-77-1

P.O. Box 1193
Escondido, CA 92025
760-489-0336
FAX 760-747-1198

Text © A. B. Curtiss 2003
Illustrations © A. B. Curtiss 2003
Printed in China
Curtiss, A. B.
        The little chapel that stood / A.B. Curtiss.–1st ed.
        p.cm.
        SUMMARY: How St. Paul's Chapel, across the street from the Twin Towers of the World Trade Center, survived the 9-11 blast and then served as a service depot for rescuers.

1. Trinity Church (New York, N. Y.).–2. New York (N.Y.)—
Church history–Juvenile literature. 3. September 11 Terrorist Attacks, 2001–Juvenile literature.
BX5980.N5C87 2003   283'.7471
ISBN 0-932529-77-1

*Dedicated to my daughter, Demming,
who encouraged me to expand my small poem
into a children's book*

The Little Chapel That Stood

by A. B. Curtiss

Illustrated by Mirto Golino

Around the Chapel
        of Old St. Paul
Blow the dancing leaves
        of the coming Fall.
In the morning breeze
        they leap and fly
Beneath the towers
        that scrape the sky.

George Washington's
    family worshiped
    here;
Alexander Hamilton's
    grave lies near.
Since Seventeen Hundred
    and Sixty Six
Has stood this house
    of God and bricks.
Solid and steadfast
    as time whirled
    around it,
Unchanged since horse
    and carriage
    found it.

A solace to presidents,
    help to the poor.
No one was ever turned
    from its door.
An immigrant's refuge,
    a sojourner's peace
Where hope is born
    and sorrows cease.

As the centuries passed,
and the city grew
dense,
Its buildings grew higher
and wider,
immense.
And tallest and grandest,
the city's great pride,
The New York
Twin Towers
rose up by its side.

The stress of power,
    the rush of people
Found comfort and rest
    beneath its steeple.
But doom, doom
    was coming
    all the time;
Doom, doom,
    to a city
    fair and fine;
Doom, doom,
    was in the planes
    that climbed;
Doom, doom,
    and then
    the sirens whined.

Two planes hi-jacked by
    a terrorist crew
Struck the Twin Towers:
    no warning, no clue!
Who thought it could
    happen,
    or knew what to do?
Firemen came and
    New York's
    Men in Blue.

Through the flying glass
        and smoke and din,
Thousands rushed out as
        these brave men
        rushed in!
On the stairwell to safety
        there was no
        stranger.
Each helped the other flee
        from the danger.
And some who
        climbed down
        remember,
        clear-cut,
The faces of firemen
        climbing up!

Elevator

And then, oh
        unthinkable
        thought!
        They fell.
One Tower, the other,
        they fell, fell, fell.
They fell with a rush
        and they fell
        with a roar.
The sky was blank where
        they'd been before.
And more was lost
        than who can say;
It was our hearts came
        down that day.
Through the clouds of
        black no one
        could see
How far spread
        this calamity.
The Giants around it
        had come
        to a fall,

But not
　　　the Chapel
　　　of Old St. Paul.
It was something
　　　of wonder,
　　　a symbol of grace,
The steeple still there,
　　　not a brick
　　　out of place.
Some say the giant
　　　sycamore wood
Had saved
　　　The Little Chapel
　　　That Stood.
The old chandeliers that
　　　they'd packed away,
Through two world wars,
　　　they did not sway.

Then the crystals
    reflected
    a busy scene
When the doors
    opened up to
    the rescue team.
There were firemen's shoes
    on the old
    iron fence,
Where they'd earlier
    hung them in haste,
    quick and tense
As they pulled on
    their boots
    and raced to
    The Towers,
Climbing melting steel
    to flaming showers.
Oh what gallant men
    did we lose
Who never came back
    to get their shoes!

Ground Zero smoldered,
     dark and grim.
Our hearts stood still,
     then we pitched in.
Helpers brought shovels,
     and pails, or pans.
If they had nothing else
     they dug
     with their hands
To clear the mountain
     of crumpled steel
From a nightmare that
     was all too real.

"New York is the greatest city
     in the world,"
     said the mayor,
     "it has the greatest
     people.
And we will never
     let a bunch
     of terrorists
     make us fearful."

Rescuers worked
    through the night
    and the day.
In the chapel they'd pause,
    then go
    on their way.
A hot cup of coffee,
    something to eat,
Here the firemen, welders,
    policemen
    would meet.
All would come to rest
    from their labor
Volunteer, doctor,
    brother, neighbor.

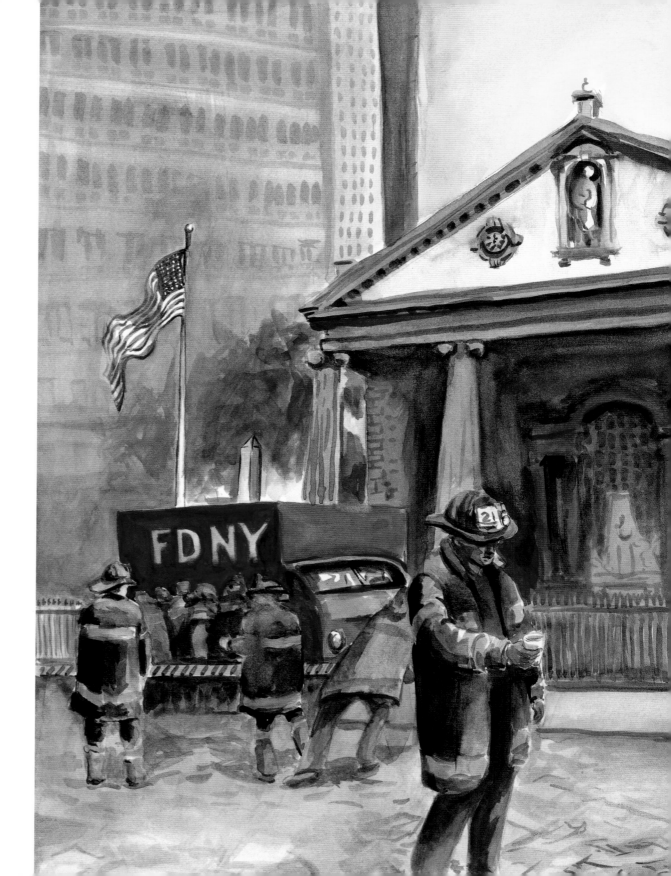

Policemen and firemen
　　led the way
But other heroes braved
　　that day.
Passengers flying
　　on Flight 93
Said, "Goodbye I love you"
　　to their family
And fought the terrorists
　　right to the ground.
Was The White House
　　where their plane
　　was bound?
We raised up the flag
　　from the dust
　　and the pain.
Freedom that's lost
　　must be won again.

Each one of us is a
        link in that chain,
To do something grand,
        or to do
        something plain.
First we take heart,
        then we take aim,
Our littlest good deed
        is never in vain.
Working together is
        how we got
        through it.
Little by little we
        learned how
        to do it.
It's nice to be big
        and it's nice
        to be tall.
But, sometimes,
        being little
Doesn't mean
        being small.

Just like the Chapel
        of Old St. Paul.

Hear the bells of freedom
        and what they say.
Terror may come
        but it will not stay.
It will shake our world
        but we will not sway.
It will block the path
        but we'll find
        our way
Free, beneath the stars
        that shine
        both night and day.